Get a Jump Start on College!

A Practical Guide for Teens

Janice Campbell

Get a Jump Start on College! A Practical Guide for Teens

Janice Campbell

A *Doing College Your Way* book.

www.GetaJumpStartonCollege.com

Published by:
Everyday Education
13041 Hill Club Lane
Ashland, Virginia 23005

www.EverydayEducation.com

© 2007 by Janice P. Campbell

Printed in the United States of America

All rights reserved. No portion of this book, except for personal copies of worksheets and forms, may be reproduced in any form without the written permission of the publisher, except for brief quotations in printed reviews.

Campbell, Janice

Get a jump start on college! / by Janice Campbell.

Includes index.

    1. Education—United States. 2. Education—Higher. 3. Education—Non-Formal Education. 4. Education—Distance Education and Learning. 5. Education—Home Schooling. I. Title.

ISBN-13: 978-0-9774685-7-7

ISBN-10: 09774685-7-7

10 9 8 7 6 5 4 3 2 1

Dedication

To my husband, Donald, whose practical wisdom anchors our family.

Thank you for your steadfast love and encouragement.

I'm looking forward to another 25 years together!

Acknowledgements

With love and gratitude to my beloved boys,

who have cheerfully been educational guinea pigs.

With gratitude to Mary Pride,

whose Big Book of Home Learning *was my constant companion*

through the early years of homeschooling, and

whose thoughtful comments strengthened this book.

And last but not least,

to the many workshop attendees over the years

who have returned to share their success stories—

you have each inspired me, and I'm grateful.

Twenty years from now

you will be more disappointed

by the things that you didn't do

than by the ones you did do.

So throw off the bowlines.

Sail away from the safe harbour.

Catch the trade winds in your sails.

Explore. Dream. Discover.

Mark Twain

Contents

Introduction 7

Early College: Why Bother? 9

What Does It Take To Earn A Degree? 15

Can You Get A Quality Education From Home? 19

    Read Widely, Learn Deeply 20

How to Earn College Credit Non-Traditionally 21

    Action Steps You Can Take Today 22

College-Level Exams 23

    ✷Smart Tip 25

Choose Your Exams 25

    Action Steps You Can Take Today 26

Portfolio Credit 27

    Action Steps You Can Take Today 32

Take a Class! 33

    Action Steps You Can Take Today 36

Choose Your College 37

Choose a Major 40

    Action Steps You Can Take Today 40

Apply For Financial Aid 41

How to Apply 42

    ✷Smart Tip 44

    Action Steps You Can Take Today   44

Create A Degree Plan   45

Skills You Need to Master   47

    Action Steps You Can Take Today   50

How to Review For College-Level Exams   51

    Study Tools   51

    Study Steps   53

Resources   55

Appendix   59

Dual-Credit Information   65

Reproducible Worksheets   67

The Jump Start Checklist   75

About the Author   79

Introduction

Imagine graduating from college with a bachelor's degree at the age when most teens are graduating from high school! When other nineteen-year-old students are taking their first college class, *you* can be choosing whether to continue with graduate work, travel for a year or so, or enter the workforce. You won't just have a head start on college— you'll have a head start on life!

I've Used These Methods...

It was in the early 1980's that I first began researching alternative education. I was interested for two reasons. First, I wanted to finish my own bachelor's degree, which I had put on hold when I got married and moved across the country, and second, I wanted to learn about homeschooling, which was just beginning to gain popularity.

Over the past couple of decades I have read nearly everything available on the subject of non-traditional education (there wasn't much in the early days!). In 2003, I put together what I had learned to complete my degree in English, using a combination of exams (over 40 credits from CLEP and DSST exams), a portfolio (6 credits), online and distance learning classes, and independent tutorials. As I worked through the process, I started sharing the good news about non-traditional ways of earning credit in workshops for people who wanted a college experience that fit their lives. Those workshops have become this book!

My Sons Have Done It...

When my first two boys hit their mid-teens and wanted more of an academic challenge, it just seemed logical for them to begin earning credit through exams and community college classes. They began by taking exams in subjects they enjoyed, and they took classes in subjects they found more difficult. They have graduated from college early, and have been very happy about their head start in life. Now, my two younger boys have started along the same path. It's an exciting thing to do!

You Can Do It Too!

This book will help you do what my sons, and countless others, have done— start earning college credit while you are still in high school. I'll start by sharing some of the advantages of getting a jump start on college, then I'll outline ways in which you can start earning credit, and finally, I'll provide some worksheets to help you plan your degree program and track your progress. You'll be amazed at just how easy it is to make the most of your high school years!

Tell Me How It's Going!

If you use the ideas in this book to get started earning college credit, I'd love to hear how it's going. You can e-mail me at jc@everydayeducation.com. If you have a special success story to share, I may even add it to the website.

Thank you for reading, and I wish you the best as you work toward your degree.

Janice Campbell

Ashland, Virginia

January 2007

Freedom is not in doing what you want to do, but in becoming what you want to be. Ardis Whitman

Early College: Why Bother?

Good Reasons for Teens and Parents

There are many advantages to earning college credit during the high school years. Students, you'll love the fact that your hard work in high school can earn a degree that is far more valuable than a high school diploma; and parents, you'll love the fact that non-traditional ways of earning college credit can save you thousands of dollars! In addition, both parents and teens can appreciate the fact that young students who are intellectually ready for a college-level challenge can study in a supportive, loving family atmosphere, rather than having to leave home before they are emotionally or spiritually mature.

Intellectual Readiness

Did you know that during the medieval era, most college students began college studies in their mid teens? There were several reasons for this, but the most significant reason is simply that most people are physically and intellectually ready to tackle challenging academic work at that age. Although most modern students pursue a far less rigorous course of study than did medieval students, they are generally capable of far more than is expected of them.

According to a history of education found in World Book Encyclopedia, "During the Middle Ages, the universities did not require students to have completed primary and secondary education to be admitted... For example, a youngster might begin attending universities at the age of 10..." Many of these students pursued studies in Latin and Greek, as well as other advanced subjects. Modern homeschoolers can choose to study challenging subjects as soon as they are ready, and best of all, they can earn credit for their hard work.

Starting college during the high school years allows the student to live and learn in a way that is developmentally appropriate...

Emotional and Academic Readiness

Teens can be intellectually ready for challenging academic work much earlier than they are emotionally, spiritually, or socially ready to move into a college setting. Doing at least a few college classes at home allows parents to continue their nurturing and mentoring roles well into the teen years, and provides students with the opportunity to discuss controversial issues and wrestle with new ideas in a warm and supportive learning environment. Starting college during the high school years allows the student to live and learn in a way that is developmentally appropriate both academically and socially.

Dual Credit

I've heard dual credit described as double-dipping, and that's really what it is, minus the germs! When you take a college class or college-level exam and earn college credit while in high school, you can also claim high school credit for the class. Students in traditional schools do this, and there is no reason homeschoolers can't.

While you can usually take college classes or exams without officially declaring dual-credit status, there can be both benefits and drawbacks to doing so. On the plus side, officially declaring dual-credit status can preserve freshman status for scholarship purposes. Also, some states or school districts will pay all or part of the tuition for dual-credit classes. On the minus side, dual-credit status sometimes comes with limits on the number of credits that may be taken, and often requires that the student register in person, rather than online.

The advantages to officially declaring dual-credit status often outweigh the negatives, so I encourage you to find out what would work best in your state and for admission to the college of your choice. I've included general information on individual state dual-credit policies in the Appendix, and you will usually find specific information on the college's website.

The Gift of Time

Students who finish college when most of their peers are finishing high school have, in effect, received a gift of four years of life. While they may choose to move directly into the workforce or into marriage as many traditional college students do, they can also choose from many other options without feeling that they need to hurry. Imagine the freedom of having a couple of years to pursue your choice of the following options:

- Volunteering / Missions
- Cultivation of a Talent / Pursuit of a Hobby
- Graduate Studies
- Entrepreneurship
- Travel

Advanced Placement

Even students who finish only a few core college courses while in high school have an advantage over their peers. They are able to skip over basic survey courses in subjects they've already completed, and study specific topics at a deeper level.

For example, as an English major, I used CLEP tests to bypass introductory courses in American and English literature so that I could fill my schedule with higher-level courses, including fascinating semester-long courses on Shakespeare, Modern Poetry, and (my favorite) Edmund Spenser's *The Faerie Queene*. My oldest son, Craig, was able to test out of survey courses in American History and Western Civilization so that he could take higher-level courses in Russian, European, and Chinese history. Neither of us would have had the time for these advanced classes if we hadn't been able to test out of the basic core classes for which we had studied on our own.

Personal Challenge and Motivation

When I look at a typical high school textbook, I can hardly blame the average teen for being disinterested in school. Not only do they have to wade through four years of tedious tidbits of knowledge, doled out piecemeal, they know that once they reach college, they'll have to go through most of the same subjects all over again. Who wouldn't feel a bit disinterested?

However, when students realize that they can earn college credit by spending just a little more time and effort on studying in high school, learning becomes much more exciting. Purposeful movement toward a challenging goal is always more interesting than passively plodding toward an easy target!

The Bottom Dollar

College isn't cheap, but there are ways to make it affordable. Non-traditional ways of earning credit can shave literally thousands of dollars from the cost of a degree.

Non-traditional ways of earning credit can shave literally thousands of dollars from the cost of a degree.

Let me share some real figures with you. I'll use numbers from real colleges in the Richmond, Virginia area that I or my boys have attended. If you'd like to check out the costs of colleges you're interested in, you can usually find tuition figures online at individual college websites.

We will compare the cost of earning one average year of credit (30 semester hours) from a public college, a private college, a community college, or by CLEP exam. I will use in-state tuition figures, which are lower than those for out-of-state students, but the costs listed will not include housing, meals, or textbooks. Most public and private universities have a flat rate for full time tuition, which is considered to be 12-19 credits. I think you'll find the numbers very interesting!

I'll leave a few spaces in the chart for you to insert figures from a few colleges of your choice, as there are substantial differences in tuition across the country. You can search for colleges on www.PrincetonReview.com, in your local phone book, or from my website, where I have a list of colleges that welcome non-traditional students. I don't think you'll find a college anywhere that can compete with the cost of college-level exams!

The Cost of 30 Credits			
Method	Sample School	Cost Per Credit	Total Cost
Community College	J. Sargeant Reynolds Community College	$80.55	$1,208.25
Public College	Virginia Commonwealth University	$179.50	$2,692.50
Private College	University of Richmond	$1,218.34	$36,550.00
Testing	CLEP- www.CollegeBoard.com	$12.50- $25.00	$375- $750
All figures are current as of June 2006.			

Notes

- The community college figure does not include miscellaneous fees such as technology fees that are included in the other college figures.

- Although the public college figure appears more inviting than the private college figure, we found (in this case at least) that the private college offered an exponentially better financial aid package that left us with almost nothing to pay, and no debt. The state school, on the other hand, had more limited aid and offered more loans, costing us a lot more out-of-pocket. I prefer private universities for many reasons!

- Variation in CLEP credit cost depends upon the number of credits (3 or 6) earned per exam. Each test costs $60 plus approximately $15 for the testing center fee. The best value is obviously the 6-credit exam!

- Isn't it amazing? Now you can see why I so highly recommend using college-level exams to get a jump start on college! It's a way to learn what you need to know without overstraining your budget, and you can do most of the work from the comfort of home. It's a win-win proposition!

The Bottom Line

- You can begin earning college credit by studying at home.

- You can start when you are ready.

- You can earn as much credit as you like.

- You can save a lot of money by doing it.

- You can get a jump-start on life by completing your degree (though not your education!) early.

- You can make the most of your high school years by going above and beyond what is normally expected of teens.

- Getting a jump-start on college is a life-changing choice you can make today!

What Does It Take To Earn A Degree?

The short answer to this is that it takes about 60 semester hours to earn an associate's degree, 120-135 hours to earn a bachelor's degree, and at least 30 more credit hours of graduate-level work to earn a master's degree. If you attend college full-time, you'll take about 15 credit hours (five average classes) per semester, and you'll most likely earn an associate's degree in two years, a bachelor's in four, and a master's in five.

Some colleges use a quarter system, in which 180 quarter hours would equal about 120 semester hours. If you need to convert quarter hours into semester hours to calculate transfer credits, just multiply the quarter hours by two-thirds. By doing this, you'll see that five-quarter-hours would equal about three-semester-hours, four quarter hours would equal 2.5 semester hours, and so forth.

Distribution of Credits

The 120-135 credits needed for a bachelor's degree must be taken to fulfil specific requirements. Let's take a look at the general distribution of credits. The credits for each class or exam taken will be applied to one of the following four categories.

- Core Curriculum
- Major Requirements
- Minor Requirements
- Electives

Some classes can fulfil the requirements of both the core and the major or minor, while other classes can be applied to only one area. You may choose more than one major or minor, if you have a broad array of interests. To begin, however, it is usually easiest to complete core requirements first, so that you can focus on your major after you are comfortable with college-level learning.

Core Curriculum

The most basic courses, sometimes known as a liberal arts core, are intended to provide a well-rounded basis for understanding the world, as well as a solid foundation for further learning. Specific core requirements are set by each college, and they vary slightly, depending upon whether the school has a liberal arts, business, or other academic focus.

Many requirements for the liberal arts core are roughly similar, though, no matter what college or university you choose. This means that you can begin planning your homeschool learning, including personal reading and activities, with the goal of earning credit through college-level exams or a portfolio even before you choose a school or major area of study.

The most basic courses, sometimes known as a liberal arts core, are intended to provide a well-rounded basis for understanding the world, as well as a solid foundation for further learning.

The Core Requirements For A Bachelor's Degree Usually Include:

6-9 semester hours English Composition

9 semester hours Humanities, which may include:

Art/Music/Drama

    Journalism/Communications

    Foreign Language

    Religion/Philosophy

9 semester hours Social Science and History, which may include:

    Anthropology/Sociology

    Psychology

    Economics

    History

9 semester hours Natural Science/Mathematics, which may include:

    Biology

    Chemistry

    Physics

    Mathematics

    Computer Science

3 semester hours Computer Skills

1-3 semester hours Health and Fitness

Note: Most classes are worth 3 credit hours. Upper level and lab courses, particularly in math, foreign language, and science, may be worth up to 5 hours.

Major and Minor Requirements

You will also need 28-36 credits to complete your major. The college you choose will have an array of disciplines from which you must choose your major. Since you will be taking at least ten classes in your major, be sure it is something you really enjoy.

My oldest son thought that accounting would be a very practical profession, so he chose it for his major. Big mistake! He loves history and music, but could quite happily face a future that didn't involve math. After three semesters of struggling through classes he didn't like, he switched his major to history, and thoroughly enjoyed the rest of his classes.

A minor is optional, but can give you the opportunity of exploring an area of special interest, and receiving credit for it. Or if you decide to change majors, you may use the credits you accumulated toward your original major as a minor, which will look better on your resume than a major plus a series of unrelated electives.

Electives

After you have completed core, major, and optional minor credits, you may choose to complete the remaining credits toward your degree by declaring a second major, a minor, or simply taking a selection of electives. An elective is, just as it sounds, a course you choose (elect) to take. It does not meet any specific degree requirements, but is taken to explore areas of interest, and to complete the number of credits required for graduation.

Can You Get A Quality Education From Home?

"No teaching, no information, becomes knowledge to any of us until the individual mind has acted upon it, translated it, transformed, absorbed it... Self education is the only possible education." Charlotte Mason

We've long since answered the question of whether or not homeschoolers could receive a high-quality K-12 education at home. Test results continually show that home-educated students stand head and shoulders above the average traditionally-schooled student, and it doesn't even depend on how they were schooled, the parent's level of education, or any of the other factors that seem relevant. Survey after survey tells the story— homeschoolers are doing well.

Is that going to change if you choose to start earning college credit from home? I don't think so! Earning college credit during the high school years doesn't seem so very intimidating once you realize that there is plenty of historical precedent for it, and that you have access to all the curriculum and tools you will need, just as you did for the K-12 years.

Read Widely, Learn Deeply

The simplest, most helpful thing you can do to increase the depth and breadth of high school learning is to read. Not casually, or simply for pleasure, but widely and deeply, from the great authors of the western literary tradition. Learn to see the connections between disciplines— to understand how literature reflects history; how geography affects economics; and how the arts mirror culture. Reading literary works that have stood the test of time is an education in itself.

If you aren't confident in your ability to select and understand the kind of literature that will create a cultivated mind, be sure to consult the Recommended Resources section for helpful foundational books. Students who have learned using Charlotte Mason's methods, *The Latin-Centered Curriculum* by Andrew Campbell, Veritas Press *Omnibus* or other classical education materials, or Sonlight Curriculum should have an excellent foundation for further study.

Are You Seeking an Education or a Credential?

Remember that education is lifelong— you won't stop learning just because you graduate. You can take the scenic route during your high school and college years and learn as much as possible, or you can move quickly through your degree plan and check off credits as rapidly as possible in order to get your degree and move on in life. Either is a valid choice, as long as you don't stop learning as soon as your diploma is in hand.

> *"The simplest, most helpful thing you can do to increase the depth and breadth of high school learning is to read. Not casually, or simply for pleasure, but widely and deeply, from the great authors of the western literary tradition."*

So teach us to number our days, that we may apply our hearts unto wisdom. Psalm 90:12

How to Earn College Credit Non-Traditionally

There are several good ways to earn college credit independently— you may mix or match according to your goals and abilities. I have earned credit using each option— exams, portfolios, and classes— and they all work well. The important thing is to start somewhere, and to end each week a little farther along than you were before.

I suggest that you read through the chapters for each method, then make some tentative decisions about the methods that will be best for your degree plan. The answers to the following self-assessment questions may help you:

Do I enjoy testing?

If you regard testing as a personal challenge, and an opportunity to measure your achievement, you would probably do well using exams to earn credit. If testing stresses you, you can choose to learn test-taking techniques from test preparation books such as Princeton Review's *Cracking* guides, and practice until you are comfortable with tests, or you may choose to use one or more of the other credit-earning options.

Have I learned or done anything at the college level for which I could assemble a portfolio of evidence to earn credit?

When I was attending Cal State Los Angeles, I earned credit for classes such as Home Management, Residential Interior Design, Horseback Riding (this was a Physical Education credit), Marriage and Family Dynamics, and Computer World (this was a long time ago, so Computer Science 280 involved a lot of interaction with the C-prompt and programming in Basic!). These are the type of topics for which you probably won't be able to earn credit by exam, so you may want to seek credit through a well-designed portfolio.

Do I need an instructor's help to get through a challenging subject?

Subjects that are difficult for you are often best approached with the help of an instructor. For me, math is very unapproachable, so it is a subject I would never study on my own. I need not only the instructor's explanations, but also the pressure of class deadlines to keep me moving. The best part of taking a difficult subject in a class is that in about 16 weeks it's over, and you don't ever have to look at it again if you don't want to!

Action Steps You Can Take Today

1. Look at the list of available college-level exams in Appendix A of this book, and check off all the exams you may want to take.

2. Make a list of subjects for which you might be able to earn portfolio credit.

3. List subjects in which you will definitely need an instructor's help.

In the next three chapters we will look at each option in more detail, so that you'll know where to begin.

College-Level Exams

College-level exams are a very efficient way to earn credit. I used them (mostly CLEP exams) to earn over 40 credits toward my bachelor's degree, and I really enjoyed the process. Imagine spending three hours in a testing center and emerging with twelve credits! I did this more than once, and it's a wonderful feeling.

These exams are also useful for:

- Demonstrating competence in a subject area.
- Filling in elective credits needed for graduation.
- Adding credibility to the grades on your high school transcript (more about this in *Transcripts Made Easy*).
- Re-earning credit for a class that didn't transfer to your four-year university.

There are several standardized tests available that offer either advanced placement or college credit in return for a satisfactory score. These include widely known exams such as the AP (Advanced Placement), SAT Subject Tests (formerly SAT II), and the CLEP (College Level Examination Program) exams, as well as lesser known tests such as DSST (formerly DANTES, now Dantes Subject Standardized Test) or TECEP (Thomas Edison State College Exam Program).

Exam Comparison Chart							
Exam	Website	Exams Available	Format	Time	Place Administered	Cost	Primary Purpose
AP	collegeboard.com	35	Pencil	3 hours	High School	$82	Placement
CLEP	collegeboard.com	34	Computer	90 min.	College	$75	Credit
SAT Subject	collegeboard.com	20	Pencil	60 min.	High School	$26-37	Placement
DSST	getcollegecredit.com	38	Pencil	Un-timed	College	$60	Credit
TECEP	www.tesc.edu	66	Pencil	2-4 hours	College	$49-98 per credit	Credit
Excelsior	www.excelsior.edu	40	Computer	2 hours	Test Center	$115-295	Credit
Remember that you can find up-to-date information and register online!							

How Do I Get Credit for Exams?

When you take a college-level exam, your results are recorded on a transcript maintained by the testing company. You can take any number of tests and they will remain on the test company's transcript for at least 20 years. When you want to apply the credit to a degree, you request that a transcript be sent to your college. Credit for all accepted exams is then recorded on the college transcript as transfer credit.

Do All Colleges Accept All Exams?

No. Most colleges accept at least some of the major exams (AP seems to be the most widely accepted and most frequently required), and some colleges even require a few of the subject exams for entrance. However, it's easy to find out whether the college of your choice accepts the exams you plan to take. Just go to the college website (you can find it by typing the college name into a search engine such as Google), or consult the college catalog. Transfer credit and exam policies should be clearly outlined, and there may even be a schedule of exam administration times.

> **✳ Smart Tip**
> If the four-year-college of your choice does not accept all the exams you want to take, try transferring your exam credit to a nearby community college (most accept CLEP, AP, and SAT Subject Exams), and take a few classes there. Your exam credit will be recorded on your community college transcript, and from there, it is often accepted as transfer credit by the four-year university. It sounds strange, but it seems to work!

Choose Your Exams

When you are ready to start taking exams, I suggest beginning with core subjects. It doesn't matter what your major will be, or what college you will attend— you will need to have a basic group of core courses in English, Math, History, and Science. Therefore, it makes sense to begin gathering those credits first.

I suggest "clustering" the subjects you are studying so that you get maximum benefit from your study time. You will notice that as you study for one subject, you inevitably pick up information useful in other areas. You can make this work to your advantage when you begin studying at the college level, because each bit of knowledge you gain makes it easier to acquire and remember related facts.

If, for example, you study for the "Introductory Psychology" exam, you will have much of the foundation and vocabulary needed to make the studying for "Educational Psychology" simpler. And after that, it's just a step or two to "Human Growth and Development."

The same principle works when studying American History. You already have a head start on the concepts and ideas in American Government as well as many of the people and places in American Literature, so you may as well go ahead and earn credit there, also. Once you start making the connections between subjects and ideas, it will make your entire study process simpler.

Suggested Subject Clusters				
Cluster 1 This is a good beginning cluster.	US History I & II	American Literature	American Government	Ethics in America
Cluster 2 My favorite cluster—good for two years of study.	Western Civilization I & II and World History	Humanities and Social Sciences & History	English Literature	Art History
Cluster 3 English Skills	Freshman Composition	Analyzing and Interpreting Literature	English Composition	Technical Writing
Cluster 4 A good choice for number crunchers!	College Mathematics and Algebra	Calculus AB and/or Calculus BC	Principles of Micro- & Macro-Economics	Financial Accounting
Cluster 5 Basic Business Skills	Introduction to Business	Introduction to Computing and Information Systems & Computer Applications	Principles of Supervision and Management Information Systems	Business Mathematics
Cluster 6 The Sciences	Biology, Chemistry, and Physics	Principles of Physical Science and/or Natural Sciences	Environment & Humanity and Here's to Your Health	Physical Geology and Astronomy

Take the Test

To register for an exam, you must first find a convenient testing center that offers the type of test you want to take. As you can see in the Exam Comparison Chart, each type of test is administered in a specific place, either a college, a high school, or a study center such as Sylvan. You can find up-to-date administration information at the websites listed for each exam, or by calling the testing center nearest you. Some exams are administered just few times a year, but others are available year-round.

Action Steps You Can Take Today

- Visit the websites listed for each type of test, and note when and where tests are administered.

- Visit the website of a college that interests you, and search for "CLEP" or "AP" to see which exams they accept.

Portfolio Credit

In order to earn credit for knowledge you've gained independently, you must be able to document that your learning has the breadth and depth you would have acquired in a college class covering similar material. While college-level exams are probably the simplest way of determining this, you may prefer to create a portfolio that will help you document your knowledge in a specific subject.

I earned six credits toward my bachelor's degree by creating a portfolio. Frankly, it was a lot more work than just taking an exam, but it allowed me to earn credit for knowledge that didn't exactly fit any of the tests available.

There are several things you'll need to remember if you plan to use a portfolio to earn credit:

- A Prior Learning Portfolio is different in purpose and scope from a year-end evaluation portfolio.
  - The year-end evaluation portfolio contains an overview of all you have covered during the year, as well as a sampling of your best work.

- The Prior Learning Portfolio contains a limited amount of information designed to show that you have met the requirements of a single class or a specific group of classes.

- You will need to choose a college that offers credit for prior learning portfolios, and has reasonable evaluation fees (you will determine this as you are filling out the College Comparison Worksheets).

- You must closely follow the instructions provided by your college for each element of the portfolio.

- You must be enrolled at a college, and create the portfolio specifically to meet the college guidelines, before you can earn credit this way.

Two Types of Portfolios

There are two types of portfolios you may be able to present for credit. The first, a 'challenge or 'class' portfolio, is the most commonly accepted. Each element in this portfolio is specifically targeted toward meeting the knowledge requirements of a single class. Occasionally, you may be able to present a portfolio that contains separate sections, with evidence of mastery for several classes in the same department. By requesting credit for more than one class at a time, you may save both time and money.

The second type of portfolio is a 'general' or 'experiential' portfolio. Rather than challenging a specific class, the contents of this portfolio simply show that you have gained knowledge or competence through experience. The experience for which credit is granted varies from school to school, but it often includes office and computer skills, or non-academic subjects such as sports. The credit granted for this type of portfolio is usually applied as elective credit, and is unlikely to apply to the requirements for your major.

Elements of a Portfolio

Most portfolios include certain basic components. I've listed them below, so that you'll have a general idea of what is required, but remember— it's *very* important to follow your own school's portfolio guidelines. Your precision and accuracy in following directions helps the portfolio evaluator to quickly move through your portfolio, compare it with the standards of the course for which you are seeking credit, and award credit if the standards are met. A portfolio that does not fit the criteria is likely to be returned without credit!

Most academic portfolios are presented in a three-ring-binder large enough to comfortably hold all the elements. Each of the following sections should be listed in the table of contents and separated by a divider tab. An art portfolio may have similar elements, but will most likely be presented in an artist's portfolio that is large enough to contain samples of artwork. Again, it's critical to follow *exactly* the instructions provided by your own college.

- **Formal Request for Evaluation:** The university may provide a specific form for this, but if not, it can be a brief letter in standard business format. It should contain:
  - Personal Identification
  - Major/Minor
  - Department or discipline from which you are requesting credit.
  - Specific course numbers for which you are requesting credit.
  - Catalog descriptions of the courses for which you are requesting credit.
  - Course names and sources of other credit you have earned in this discipline.
- **Table of Contents**
- **Resume or Curriculum Vitae (CV)**
- **Description of Learning**
  - A formal narrative that describes what you have learned, how you learned it, and how the knowledge you have acquired is equivalent to the knowledge that would be gained in the class you are challenging.
- **Formal Request for Credit**
  - This is usually a specific form provided by the university, but it can also be an essay or letter, depending upon the college's requirements.
- **Appendices**

Each element of documentation, including work samples and letters of verification, will be housed in a separate appendix in the portfolio. Each appendix will be identified by letters— Appendix A, Appendix B, and so forth.

How to Put it Together

Four questions to help you decide if your knowledge qualifies for portfolio credit:

If you were attending college on campus, could you take a class in this subject?

Can you see the big-picture concepts related to the topic?

Is your knowledge or skill usable in more than one situation?

Do you understand the theory that underlies your skill?

Before you begin to create a portfolio, you need to talk to the guidance counselor at the school where you hope to obtain the credit. First, verify that the college accepts the type of portfolio you plan to do, and that it fits into your degree plan. Second, request a copy of the college's portfolio guidelines, and any forms you may need to include. Third, request a copy of the syllabus for the class you plan to challenge. Finally, ask if there are sample portfolios available to look at. A sample is worth a thousand words!

If you are doing a challenge portfolio, use the class syllabus, along with your guidance counselor's instructions, to determine what papers and documentation you need to include. For an experiential portfolio, follow the directions provided in the college guidelines. Assemble the elements of the portfolio, and place them in order in a three-ring binder, or other folder, as instructed. Write the Description of Learning, including references to supporting materials in your appendices.

For example, your description of learning may say something like this: "The website I created for XYZ Company was awarded first place in the Webby Functionality Contest (see related documentation in Appendix G)." In Appendix G, you would place a copy of the certificate, if you have one, along with copies of any related news articles or letters of commendation. Use only the most relevant items, so you don't overwhelm the evaluator!

When you feel that the portfolio is complete, make sure that you have included each element in the order requested by the college guidelines. Be sure to ask someone else to proofread it, so that it will be free of typos and other small errors. Print two copies; keep one for your personal file, and turn in the other copy, along with payment for the evaluation. You will usually find out within four to six weeks whether credit has been granted.

Is It College-Level Learning?

As you consider seeking credit for a portfolio, you need to be sure that the knowledge for which you hope to earn credit is actually college-level learning. College-level knowledge differs from high-school learning just as a Rembrandt painting differs from a child's pencil sketch. Colleges will not grant credit for high-school work!

When you have learned American history at the high-school level, for example, you can probably provide a rough chronology of major events and the people who participated in them (or maybe not!). Once you understand the same material at the college-level, you will know not just the chronological outline, but also many of the details that paint an interesting and memorable picture. More importantly, you will also understand the underlying causes of events and be able to apply that understanding to analysis and interpretation of current events.

If you aren't sure whether your knowledge is college level, the following questions may help you decide:

- If you were attending college on-campus, could you take a class in this subject?
    - One of the easiest ways to find out whether a class is offered at the college level is to request a catalog (or check the online catalog on a college's website) from one or more colleges. You can also use the catalog to gather ideas on how to list and title the courses for which you plan to seek portfolio credit.
- If you are seeking credit for knowledge you've gained on the job, do you understand the overall concepts that tie together individual tasks?
    - If you have a lot of practical experience, but are not able to articulate the theories that underlie your knowledge, you probably need to do some reading in your field so that you will understand the "why's" of the topic. For example, if you are seeking credit for advertising copywriting, you need to be able to explain the marketing and psychological principles that must be applied for ad copy to be successful.
- Is the knowledge or skill usable in other job situations?
    - A skill that is specific to a single employer is not likely to be broad enough for college credit.

- If you hope to obtain credit for hobby or volunteer activities, can you document reading or activities you've done that have contributed to your understanding of the theory and practice of your skill? For example, music instruction should include theory and performance in order to be considered college level. A good bibliography, samples of work completed, or a letter of verification from someone who knows your skills can be a valuable addition to your portfolio.

Action Steps You Can Take Today

- Go to your college website for specific instructions on what to include in a portfolio, and how to format it.

- Start keeping materials that you can use in the portfolio.

- Write letters to teachers, coaches, mentors, ministers, or employers, requesting transcripts or a letter confirming your achievements.

Take a Class!

There are some subjects that are just easier to learn with an instructor. Complex subjects such as calculus or physics, or subjects for which you need specialized equipment, such as the lab sciences or some of the applied arts, are good choices for taking with an instructor. You can choose to take classes online, or by traditional distance learning, or at a local campus.

Online and Distance Learning Classes

All you have to do is turn on your computer and search for "online college classes" and you will be inundated with options. Countless universities have realized that the non-traditional student body is growing dramatically, and they're falling all over themselves to fill the needs of this new market. My website offers links to several directories of colleges that offer online and distance learning options. You may also visit sites such as www.Petersons.com to search for a college that offers the classes you want to take. Remember to always check the accreditation for any school you are considering!

Online and distance learning classes work pretty much like traditional classes, except that in place of classroom lectures, you have assigned reading. In some classes you "attend" audio or video lectures, or participate in message board or forum discussions. You usually communicate with your professor via e-mail or an online message board system. Online classes usually have some offline reading and assignments, and distance learning classes often have online components. Computers have become so ubiquitous that they are an integral part of almost all types of college-level learning!

I enjoyed the online and distance learning classes I took because:

- The syllabus provided a detailed outline of all that is to be covered so that I knew the big picture from the first day of the semester and could budget my time wisely.

- I had more direct communication with professors through e-mail than I ever did in a classroom.

- Classwork scheduling seemed more flexible than in a traditional classroom. Because I didn't have go anywhere or be online at a specific time, I could work whenever and wherever was convenient.

- Completion of many online research assignments meant that computer competence was an almost inevitable by-product of taking distance-learning classes.

The least expensive option for college-level classes is usually a community college. These "colleges with training wheels" are becoming accustomed to welcoming homeschoolers, and many have policies posted on their websites, outlining exactly what homeschooled students must do in order to take classes. All my boys began taking classes at a community college when they were in their mid-teens, and they found it a very businesslike way to earn credit, and all the credit they earned transferred easily to their four-year universities.

I feel that community colleges can be an excellent option for homeschoolers because:

- The student body tends to be composed of older, more serious students than the average residential college.

- There is virtually no social life to distract students from learning.

- This type of college is geared toward transitional and first-generation college students, so it is equipped to provide extra help or academic support services as needed.

- It is very easy to become a part-time student at a community college, and you can take a class or two without a long-term commitment.

- It's a good introduction to formal classroom procedures in a relatively low-stakes setting.

Local Four-Year Universities

Some colleges allow community members to take classes on a space-available basis, usually at a rate that is discounted from their usual tuition. You should be able to find out if your local college offers this option by visiting their website or calling the admissions department.

Taking a few classes at an accredited four-year university can be a wonderful opportunity to experience a real college setting without committing to a long-term relationship. I don't recommend starting with this option, though, because a four-year university is a challenging and academically intense experience. It would probably be best to try this after you have accumulated some credit using other options.

Action Steps You Can Take Today

If You Want To Take A Few Classes

- Request catalogs from your local community colleges as well as some accredited distance learning schools.

- Look at college websites to find out how homeschoolers can enroll in classes.

- Fill out and send the application for enrollment, either online or on paper.

- Choose one or more classes you'd like to take, and register for them online.

- Buy the recommended textbooks through the college bookstore or through online booksellers such as www.Amazon.com.

Choose Your College

The process of choosing a college where you can earn credit non-traditionally is somewhat different from choosing a college for traditional learning. Some things remain the same, however. You must still determine whether the school is accredited, and what your basic costs will be. In addition, you need to select a college that allows you to earn credit in the non-traditional ways you may want to use.

If you plan to earn your degree entirely at home, and you want to make extensive use of exams, you need to plan ahead and choose a college that welcomes credit earned through testing. You can begin your search for a test-friendly college by looking at the exam websites (listed in each exam description in the table on page 18) for lists of colleges that accept some or all of the exams. You may also visit the website, www.DoingCollegeYourWay.com, where you'll find an ever-evolving list of colleges that welcome non-traditional students. You can click on those that sound interesting and request free information, which will help you to make wise decisions.

If you are simply planning to earn a year or two worth of credit before entering a traditional university, just verify that the schools you are considering will accept transfer credit earned through testing or portfolios. Most colleges will accept course credit from other accredited universities, but they can choose whether to apply the credit to core or major requirements or to simply use it as elective credit.

Why is Accreditation Important?

I've mentioned accreditation a couple of times, and you may be wondering exactly why it matters. According to the U.S. Department of Education, "the goal of accreditation is to ensure that education provided by institutions of higher education meets acceptable levels of quality" (www.ed.gov/admins/finaid/accred/index.html?src=qc). While accreditation alone can't guarantee that you'll get a good education, it can ensure that the credits you earn will be transferable, and the degree that you end up with will be respected by prospective employers, or by graduate schools if you decide to continue your education. If you neglect to make sure your college is accredited, you may find that you have done a lot of work, and spent a lot of money for a degree that is worthless. Always verify accreditation!

"You don't have to choose your major before you start earning credit — just begin with basic core classes in language arts, math, history, and science. As you work through the basics, you'll learn more about what interests you..."

There are six regional accrediting agencies (see Resources), plus a number of specialized agencies that grant accreditation to specific departments or programs. There is even an agency, the Transnational Association of Christian Colleges and Schools (TRACS), that oversees the accreditation of Christian colleges. Each legitimate accrediting agency (beware of fake ones!) is recognized by the U.S. Department of Education or the Council for Higher Education Accreditation (CHEA). You can find a lot of information, including links to each of the legitimate accrediting agencies and searchable databases of accredited schools at the following websites:

- U.S. Department of Education- www.ed.gov
- CHEA- www.chea.org
- TRACS- www.tracs.org

Using the College Comparison Worksheet

To help you think through important considerations in choosing a college that will grant non-traditional credit, the College Comparison Worksheet (found in the Reproducible Worksheets section) makes it easy for you to summarize the information you receive from the various schools and compare one school with another.

The worksheet provides space to write information in the four basic areas you will need to consider:

• College information—the name, location, and contact information of the school you are considering. Remember that in-state tuition is usually cheaper than out-of-state tuition, so location matters a little bit, even though you may never actually go to the campus.

• Admissions information—the basic requirements for admission for non-traditional students. Will you need to produce SAT or ACT scores, a high school transcript, or take placement tests? Most colleges with a non-traditional degree program make the admissions process fairly simple—they know we don't have time for jumping through a lot of hoops!

• Types of credit accepted by the college. This will tell you how many options you have for completing your degree at this school. Do they accept transfer credits from other colleges? Life-experience portfolios? Credit by exam?

• Financial information—how much it will cost you. This is an important piece of the college puzzle. Please don't make assumptions without making a written comparison of all the figures! You can't assume, for example, that private colleges will always cost more than public colleges, or that you will not qualify for federal financial aid. You simply cannot know this until you have filled out the worksheets and the Free Application for Federal Student Aid (FAFSA).

When I filled out the financial information part of the form for myself, I was shocked to discover that the small, private women's college that I was certain would be financially impossible was actually the most affordable for me. I was thrilled that my first-choice school was a reasonable alternative, but I would have never applied there if I hadn't first filled out this worksheet. So—fill out this worksheet for every single college that interests you. Who knows? Maybe the school of your dreams is within your reach.

Choose a Major

Choosing a major is a big step, and in some cases, knowing the subject you want to major in can help you decide on the college that is right for you. Your choice of a major will reflect your interests and career plans. If you're not sure what you want to do, I suggest taking some aptitude tests and reading books such as *Do What You Are* and *What Color is Your Parachute?* (See complete information on these books in the Recommended Resources section.)

You don't have to choose your major before you start earning credit, though—just begin with basic core classes in language arts, math, history, and science. As you work through the basics, you'll learn more about what interests you, and what might be the best field for you to pursue. If you are undecided about your major, try taking a class in each of the disciplines you are considering. It may help you decide, and you will be earning credit that can be applied toward your degree.

Action Steps You Can Take Today

- Visit college websites and research their homeschool policies, accreditation status, tuition amounts, and testing policies.

- Request more information from colleges that interest you.

- Learn more about accreditation through the websites mentioned, or by reading *Bears' Guide to Earning Degrees by Distance Learning*. (See the Resources chapter for details.)

- Check out books from the library on choosing colleges. One I particularly like is Loren Pope's *Colleges That Change Lives*.

- Check out and read *Do What You Are* and other books that can help you learn more about your aptitudes and abilities.

- Make a list of people you know who do interesting work. Ask each of them if you can shadow them for a day or two to learn more about their career.

Apply For Financial Aid

"You miss 100% of the shots you never take." Wayne Gretzky

There are many good books on financial aid, so I won't cover it exhaustively here. The main thing you need to know is that most people will qualify for some form of aid, and the only bad thing you can do related to financial aid is to fail to apply for it. It never hurts to try, and you may be surprised by what you are offered!

Beware of the Temptation to Make Assumptions!

- Do not assume that you make too much money to qualify for aid.
- Do not assume that a state school will be less expensive than a private school.
- Do not assume that you have to have perfect grades to qualify for aid.

These assumptions can cost you a lot of money! First of all, aid is awarded based on considerations other than need. Second, private schools usually have substantial endowments that enable them to provide generous grants. Third, scholarships can be based upon many things other than merit, including ethnicity, career goals, and special circumstances. When you fill out the questionnaire at scholarship search websites such as FastWeb, you will get an idea of what I mean. There are scholarships from virtually every special-interest group you can imagine!

How to Apply

The FAFSA

The first step in applying for financial aid is to fill out the Free Application for Federal Student Aid (FAFSA) at www.fafsa.ed.gov. Be sure to visit only the official FAFSA site with the ".ed.gov" suffix. There are other sites that use the acronym "fafsa" with other suffixes, but these are not the official government site. Filing the FAFSA is free, so if you are at a site that requests a payment for processing your application, you are not at the official site.

You need to have your banking and income tax information at hand in order to complete the application. When you arrive at the website, you will be able to download and print a "FAFSA on the Web Worksheet." If you go through this worksheet and complete all the questions, filling out the actual application on line will take very little time, even with a dial-up connection. You will receive a Personal Identification Number (PIN) that will allow you to view your application, make corrections, and fill out future applications without re-entering basic identification data.

EFC: The Number that Matters

When you submit the online FAFSA, you will receive an estimate of your Estimated Family Contribution (EFC). The difference between this amount and the cost of the college is known as your *need*. Colleges will look at the EFC figure, then subtract it from their total tuition and expenses to come up with a total financial aid package, which they will present to you in a offer letter.

For example, if your EFC is $1,500, and you are looking at schools with yearly costs of $8,000 and $25,000, you can expect the first school to offer an aid package of $6500 and the second school to offer a package of $23,500. The aid package will usually consist of a combination of grants, scholarships, loans, and work study, and you will have the opportunity to compare aid packages and select the one that best meets your needs.

Other Scholarships and Grants

After you submit your FAFSA, go to www.fastweb.com or www.scholarships.com and fill out a scholarship profile. These search engines match the data you enter with available scholarships and contests and e-mail you information about scholarships for which you may qualify. Factors that scholarship committees consider include:

- Grades
- Citizenship
- Quality of Essay
- Geographical Location
- Ancestry
- Parent's Field of Work
- Parent or Grandparent's Military Service
- And much more!

It's possible to earn quite a bit of money from scholarships and essay contests if you have the perseverance to collect all the information for the application. One of the smartest things you can do to increase your chances of earning scholarship money is to apply for small local scholarships. There are hundreds, even thousands, of dollars that go unclaimed each year because no one applied for the scholarship. You can find out about local scholarships through your college advisor, or even through other college websites. It is certainly worth a try, because your chances for winning are relatively high.

For a bit of inspiration, you may want to read *How to Go to College Almost for Free*, where you'll discover how Benjamin Kaplan accumulated nearly $90,000 in scholarship funds for his education at Harvard. It can be done!

What About Freshman-Only Scholarships?

If you earn a lot of college credit while in high school, it may make you ineligible for freshman-only scholarships at some universities. For the average student, this may not matter much, as these scholarships tend to go to outstanding students or athletes, and the amount you can save using *Jump Start* methods is often just as much as you might have received if you won a freshman-only scholarship. If you are planning to go into a community college, or if you have been accepted into a college that covers the entire amount of a student's financial need without regard to whether the student is a freshman or a transfer student, you probably don't need to worry about freshman-only scholarships at all.

If you are an outstanding student, and you want to be eligible for freshman-only scholarships, you can often take advantage of dual-credit status to retain freshman standing for financial aid purposes. In addition, you can take AP and CLEP exams, then wait to have the exam transcript sent to your college until after you have been accepted and completed the first semester or two. Visit college websites to see what scholarships are available, and what the eligibility requirements are, so that you can proceed confidently.

> **✳ Smart Tip**
> Be sure to keep copies of all the essays you write for college admissions and scholarship competitions. Many scholarship committees request essays on generic topics such as "What are your goals? or "What obstacles have you overcome in seeking your education?" This means that you can write and polish one or two standard essays, and make them work for several occasions just by personalizing the details to fit specific competitions.

- Gather your most recent bank statements and income tax return.
- Fill out the online FAFSA to see what your EFC might be.
- Fill out scholarship search databases so that you can start learning about scholarship opportunities.
- Visit the websites of college you may be considering, and find out what kinds of financial aid they offer, and what percentage of their students receive financial aid.

Create A Degree Plan

If you want to earn your entire degree at home, you'll need to create a Degree Plan. This is an outline of the credits you need to earn to complete your degree, along with a tentative plan for how each credit will be earned. Once you begin taking exams or classes and working toward your degree, you will record on the form a brief note about how each requirement was actually fulfilled, along with your grades or exam scores. This enables you to see at a glance what you've accomplished and how much you have left to do, and ensures that you do not miss any classes that are critical to your graduation. Think of it as the road map to your destination!

Although your college advisor may create a degree plan for you, I highly recommend that you fill out and maintain your own plan. I suggest this for several reasons:

- You are the person most concerned with your education, so you will be most likely to invest the time necessary to achieve your goals in a timely and efficient way.

- Your advisor has many students to consider, and cannot focus solely on your needs. He or she can answer your questions and help you plan, but you will need to choose classes for each semester, and verify that all requirements are met, so that you don't come up short right before graduation. One of my sons ended up having to take an extra class because his advisor had mistakenly told him that a class he had already taken would fulfill a specific requirement, and it did not. If you "own" your degree plan, you should be able to spot problems before they occur!

• If you know exactly what you need to study, you can plan your classes for maximum efficiency. You can schedule English history and English literature for the same semester, for example, as discussed in the "clustering" section of the Exams chapter, so that the overlapping areas of study can decrease your study time while enhancing learning.

• Knowing exactly what you need to take will enable you to schedule prerequisites when they are needed, so that you don't encounter unexpected obstacles.

• Planning ahead makes a large task seem less overwhelming.

• The joy of checking off each requirement as you complete it can reinforce your sense of accomplishment and keep you moving forward.

To fill out the Degree Plan worksheet found in the "Reproducibles" section, use your college catalog to fill in the core requirements, major requirements, minor requirements (optional), and elective credits. You will need about four copies of this worksheet in order to hold all the classes you need to take for a bachelor's degree. Remember, 120 credits is equal to about forty classes.

Skills You Need to Master

"..the tools of learning are the same, in any and every subject; and the person who knows how to use them will, at any age, get the mastery of a new subject in half the time with a quarter of the effort expended by the person who has not the tools at his command." Dorothy Sayers

Miss Sayers was talking about the classical tools of the trivium, which you may read more about in her helpful essay, "The Lost Tools of Learning," which is reprinted in Douglas Wilson's book *Recovering the Lost Tools of Learning*. The skills I've listed here are other skills you'll need in college, and they too will smooth the path of learning. I do want to emphasize that you don't need to master these things *before* starting college-level work. You'll learn them by doing them in the course of your assignments.

Essay and Research Report Writing

You need excellent composition skills; practice in both timed and untimed essay and report writing; and an understanding of the most commonly used methods of citation, as outlined below. A basic handbook such as *Write for College* provides instructions for researching, writing, revising, and proofreading various types of essays, as well as help in developing the skills listed as Writing Basics.

Writing Basics You Need to Know
- The five-paragraph essay.
- The Five-Step Writing Process–
  - Read / Research
  - Think on Paper (brainstorming)
  - Organize Ideas
  - Write
  - Revise
- How to use writing handbooks and research materials.

Citations

I recommend learning the following citation methods which are required for various types of classes:

- MLA (Modern Language Association)- This method of in-text citations seems to be most often used in literature and other humanities classes. I find it the most simple and logical method of citation, and it seems to be growing in popularity.

- APA (American Psychological Association)- Another method of in-text citation that is usually required in the social sciences.

- *Chicago Manual of Style*- This is a citation system, using footnotes and endnotes, that is often used in history and humanities classes.

Online Research:

This is an essential component of any education. You must learn to conduct specific searches, select credible sources, and correctly cite information you use. Online research can save astonishing amounts of time and money, but like traditional research, can be done badly. Research can seem easy with the internet, but you must still check facts and avoid plagiarism. Never just cut and paste from the information you find online!

Credible Research Resources
- Databases offered through your local or college library

- Encyclopedia sites (though information is usually very general)
- Sites hosted by colleges (URL ends in .edu)

Personal Organization

It is helpful to keep a three-ring binder for each subject you study and each class you take. Put in the class syllabus and schedule, plus copies of all your notes and written assignments. That way, everything related to the subject stays together and is organized for easy review. I like to use plastic sheet protectors, so that I don't have to punch holes in every sheet of paper.

Time Management

If you are old enough to do college level work, you are old enough to plan your time wisely. Learn to look at project due dates and create intermediate deadlines for each step of a project so that you don't find yourself cramming at the last minute, or turning in an inferior essay because you didn't start soon enough.

If you need to learn time-management skills, you may want to look at Sean Covey's *Seven Habits of Highly Effective Teens* or Julia Morganstern's *Time Management from the Inside Out*.

Test-Taking Skills

There are techniques you can use to increase your chances for success on a standardized test. These include knowing how to manage time, understanding the best way to approach multiple choice questions, having a game plan for timed essays, and understanding the scoring system for the type of test you are taking. Other books in the *Doing College Your Way* series will address these points in more detail, but be aware that these are skills you will need to learn and practice for maximum success.

Be sure to take one or more sample exams from a test-prep book before you take a real college-level exam. That way, there will be few surprises, and you will feel much more confident when taking the real thing! For the most part, I suggest using the test-prep books published by the company that publishes the exams. The sample problems they offer seem to be most like the questions on the tests.

Action Steps You Can Take Today

- Assess your current skills in the areas you must master. Your parents or other adults may be able to help you decide whether you are ready to begin studying at a higher level.

- If you need help in any of the specific skill areas, check out the recommended resources from the library, and begin working on what you need to know.

- Remember, you will learn a lot by doing your college-level assignments, so don't wait for mastery before you start. Begin as soon as possible!

How to Review For College-Level Exams

Is there a good way to study and review for CLEP, AP, DSST, and SAT Subject Tests? Absolutely! The best thing you can bring to any learning situation or exam is a long history of thoughtful reading and study (use book lists from Veritas Press or Sonlight Curriculum, if you don't know where to start). Once you have studied a subject using real books and relevant audio and video resources, you can prepare for the exam by reviewing with the following tools and techniques.

Study Tools

College Textbook

The college text will serve as your scope and sequence as you study a subject at college level. Choose a reasonably current edition (with the exception of anthologies, where older is often better) with an abundance of charts and graphs, and helpful features such as chapter overviews, previews, reviews, and so on. Brand-new college texts are very expensive, with many over $100. It makes a lot of sense to buy used copies from online retailers such as Amazon.com, Half.com, or other bookstores.

Core Reading

Select core reading materials to go with each chapter of the text. These may include biographies of important people, atlases for locating significant geographic features, historical fiction featuring the time and place you're studying, relevant literary works, such as poetry and drama, reports from scientific journals, and anything else that helps to bring the subject to life. You don't need to select all the materials ahead of time— just pick enough to get started, and add more as you go along.

Audio and Video Resources

Check your library for audio and video resources that will help you learn your topic. BBC and PBS documentaries can be particularly helpful for history and the sciences, and the BBC productions of Shakespeare's plays are among the best. The Teaching Company, www.teach12.com, offers complete college courses on audio and video. We own many of them, and they are extremely well done, and excellent, not only for test preparation, but also for in-depth learning.

Notebook

A college-ruled spiral-bound notebook is easiest to handle, but a three-ring binder allows you to keep all papers from all your classes in one place. Just choose whichever you prefer.

Timeline

For humanities classes, a timeline helps place people and events into chronological context. The timeline I designed for this purpose and have used for years—*Time-Frame Timeline*—will be available as an e-book from my website soon (depending on when you're reading this, it may already be available). It's an indispensable tool for teen and adult visual learners!

Index Cards and File

Record significant details of one important concept, event, or person per card. Use them as flash cards before the exam (write name or event on the back, and see how many of the details you can remember just by seeing the name of the concept, person, or event), then file them alphabetically in your card file as a permanent supplement to the brief information on your timeline.

Study Steps

- Preview the college textbook by scanning the table of contents (notice that it is in outline format), then scan the rest of the book, looking at the learning objectives, photos, charts, graphs, and chapter reviews. Get an idea of the scope of your subject, and the sequence in which it is covered.

- Turn to the first assigned chapter of your textbook or literature anthology, and skim the entire chapter, slowing down to read parts that seem especially important. If you are an auditory learner, it may help your concentration if you read aloud.

- Begin reading core reading materials, and using any audio or video resources you've gathered. Take notes as you read, using the timeline and index cards as described below, and analyzing how each resource ties into the textbook chapter.

- Focus on discovering and analyzing the most important points covered in the chapter (usually the things mentioned more than once, especially those mentioned in chapter subheads and the review section).

- Feel free to mark significant passages in your books (unless you're working with a library book, of course).

- If you are studying history, art, or literature, record important people and events on your timeline and index cards.

- For mathematics and science classes, record important concepts from the book on your index cards, and work some of the problems. Many college instructors assign about half the odd or even problems in each lesson. They prefer to see a few perfectly solved problems than many problems badly done.

- As you finish each chapter, review the timeline and index card entries.

- At your next study session, use your notebook to record the main points you recall from the text, then open the text book and see what you have left out. Go through the chapter and fill in your notes, creating a mini-outline or narrative. For math, check your problems and rework as necessary, moving on when you feel confident.

- Continue to study each chapter in this way, reviewing your timeline and index cards regularly as you work through the text.

- When you complete the textbook, schedule your exam and continue to review your text and notes until the exam.

Never regard your study as a duty,

but as the enviable opportunity

to learn to know the liberating influence of beauty

in the realm of the spirit

for your own personal joy

and to the profit of the community

to which your later work belongs.

Albert Einstein

Resources

Adler, Mortimer, and Charles Van Doren. *How to Read a Book*. New York: Touchstone, 1972. There's a lot more to reading than just decoding. Adler and Van Doren's classic work on reading will help you begin to understand different ways of reading and the importance of reading well. Very helpful!

Bar Charts. These laminated *Quick Study* guides are very useful as a scope and sequence for what is covered in an academic subject at the college level. These inexpensive study aids can be found in many book stores, as well as online at www.barcharts.com. They contain quite a bit of information, but don't imagine that you could pass the test just by memorizing all the facts on a chart. It's just an overview, and there is a lot more to learn!

Barnes & Noble Online University- http://university.barnesandnoble.com. Barnes & Noble offers free online courses on many different topics. Many would be suitable for supplementary work as part of self-directed study. 2006 offerings include courses on German, grammar, opera, the poetry of Emily Dickenson, Shakespeare's tragedies, beginning programming, organizing, and much more.

Bauer, Susan Wise. *The Well-Educated Mind: A Guide to the Classical Education You Never Had*. New York: W. W. Norton & Company, 2003. Though it's written primary for adults, Bauer's guide is an excellent resource for students doing college independently. She focuses on five types of great literature, and offers guidance for understanding each genre.

Bear, John, and Mariah P. Bear. *Bears' Guide to Earning Degrees by Distance Learning*. Berkeley, CA: Ten Speed Press, 2003 (or most current edition). This book is a very opinionated guide to choosing an appropriate college for your non-traditional degree. It also offers exhaustive coverage of the accreditation issue. I've read several editions of it, and I find it more interesting, and possibly more useful, than the Peterson's Guide.

Bolles, Richard Nelson. *What Color Is Your Parachute: A Practical Manual for Job-Hunters and Career-Changers*. Berkeley, CA: Ten Speed Press, 2005 (or most current edition).

Campbell, Janice. *Transcripts Made Easy: Your Friendly Guide to High School Paperwork, 3rd Edition*. Ashland, VA: Everyday Education, 2007. You'll want to create a professional-looking transcript and diploma for your student, and this book will walk you through the process. You'll also find reproducible worksheets for record-keeping. www.TranscriptsMadeEasy.com

College Board. *CLEP Official Study Guide*. Current edition. This guide is useful for its sample tests and for its detailed breakdown of the information covered in each exam. The publisher suggests that if you can get half the questions correct on one of the sample exams, you can probably pass the real test. Frankly, I prefer a larger margin, so I suggest waiting to take the exam until you can get at least 70% of the sample questions correct.

College Board. *The Official Study Guide for the SAT* offers several full-length exams, plus excellent explanations of the logic behind each type of question. It also includes samples of student essays, with an analysis of how they were evaluated. You will most likely need to take the SAT before transferring to a four-year university, so you should definitely work through this guide before test day.

Covey, Sean. *The Seven Habits of Highly Effective Teens*. New York: Fireside, 1998. It's a good idea to learn good time and life management habits during the teen years, and Covey's book provides solid, practical advice on how to focus on what's really important, so that you can accomplish the things you most want to do in life. Parents may prefer to read the classic *Seven Habits of Highly Effective People* by Sean's father, Stephen Covey.

Cowan, Louise, and Os Guiness, eds. *Invitation to the Classics: A Guide to Books You've Always Wanted to Read*. Grand Rapids, Michigan: Baker Books, 1998. This is a gentle introduction to the authors and literary works that are central to understanding Western Civilization. I reference this book in my *Zeitgeist Literature* series.

Intercollegiate Studies Institute - www.isi.org. An Internet Resource Center with excellent resources, including articles, audio and video lectures, and a college guide, designed to promote and support "a free and virtuous society." Their *Guides to the Major Disciplines* are helpful, interesting introductions to each of the major fields of study.

Perdue University's Online Writing Lab (OWL) - http://owl.english.purdue.edu. This terrific resource offers style guides for MLA and APA citations, free writing consultations, and an enormous amount of high-quality information.

Peterson's Guide to Distance Learning Programs. Lawrenceville, NJ: Thomson Peterson's, 2005 (or most current edition). This catalog provides a straightforward listing of distance learning programs. It's an alternative to Bears' Guide if you prefer your lists to be unopinionated. Much of the information is available online at www.Petersons.com.

Princeton Review Test Guides. Princeton Review publishes well-designed exam review books with particularly good test-taking tips and techniques. I suggest using these as a supplement to the guides published by the companies that create the exams. For some subjects, the sample test questions in these guides seemed harder than those on the actual test, but for other subjects the questions were significantly easier. The "official" guides contain questions written by the test creators, so they are the best way to measure readiness.

Rosetta Stone Language Courses. These multi-sensory language courses are not only simple to use, they are amazingly effective. Whatever language you'd like to learn, Rosetta Stone probably has a course!

Sebranek, Meyer, Kemper. *Write for College: A Student Handbook*. Massachusetts: Write Source, 1997. A useful handbook from the publishers of Writers Inc. It offers specific instructions for various types of writing, plus actual student writing samples (some of which are not very good, though quite realistic).

Strunk, William, and E. B. White. *The Elements of Style* (any edition). This little classic will help you develop a clear, concise writing style. I recommend reading it about once a year.

The Teaching Company - www.Teach12.com. If you could take classes from the best professors in the country, and listen to their interesting lectures as many times as you like, it would be a snap to get a jump start on college. You *can* do it with the audio and video courses offered by The Teaching Company! Our family has been buying courses from this company for years, and they are excellent. I highly recommend them.

Tieger, Paul D., and Barbara Barron-Tieger. *Do What You Are: Discover the Perfect Career for You Through the Secrets of Personality Type*. New York: Little, Brown, 2001. This helpful guide uses a personality assessment to provide targeted career suggestions.

Regional Accrediting Agencies

- Middle States Association of Colleges and Schools- www.msche.org
- New England Association of Schools and Colleges- www.neasc.org
- North Central Association of Colleges and Schools- www.ncacihe.org
- Northwest Association of Schools and Colleges- www.nwccu.org
- Southern Association of Colleges and Schools- www.sacs.org
- Western Association of Colleges and Schools- www.wascweb.org

Appendix

Here are a few things to help you decide which exams to take, and whether dual-credit status would be beneficial for you. Remember that this is just a starting point— you will need to get specific information from the schools you choose to work with.

Available Exams

These are the major standardized exams available at the time of printing. You can use this list to help create your Degree Plan. As you can see, it's not hard to find enough exams for at least a couple years of college credit! Even if you decide not to use exams for credit, taking a few of them will add a lot of credibility to the grades on your high school transcript. If you can pass a college-level exam, you have obviously studied the subject well.

Remember to check the test creator's website (found in the chart on page 24) for details on what is covered in each exam, information on where and when to register, and test-taking tips and resources. The testing companies want you to succeed, so they provide a lot of useful information!

CLEP- College Level Exam Program

Composition and Literature

- * American Literature
- * Analyzing and Interpreting Literature
- * English Composition
- * English Literature
- * Freshman College Composition
- * Humanities

Foreign Languages

- * French Language (Levels 1 and 2)
- * German Language (Levels 1 and 2)
- * Spanish Language (Levels 1 and 2)

History and Social Sciences

- * American Government
- * Human Growth and Development
- * Introduction to Educational Psychology
- * Introductory Psychology
- * Introductory Sociology
- * Principles of Macroeconomics
- * Principles of Microeconomics
- * Social Sciences and History
- * U.S. History I: Early Colonizations to 1877
- * U.S. History II: 1865 to the Present
- * Western Civilization I: Ancient Near East to 1648
- * Western Civilization II: 1648 to the Present

Science and Mathematics

* Biology

* Calculus

* Chemistry

* College Algebra

* College Mathematics

* Natural Sciences

* Precalculus

Business

* Financial Accounting (New in 2007)

* Introductory Business Law

* Information Systems and Computer Applications

* Principles of Accounting (To be replaced by Financial Accounting in 2007.)

* Principles of Management

* Principles of Marketing

DSST- Dantes Subject Standardized Tests

Mathematics

- Fundamentals of College Algebra
- Principles of Statistics

Social Science

- Art of the Western World
- Western Europe since 1945;
- An Introduction to the Modern Middle East
- Human/Cultural Geography
- Rise and Fall of the Soviet Union
- A History of the Vietnam War

- The Civil War and Reconstruction
- Foundations of Education
- Lifespan Developmental Psychology
- General Anthropology
- Drug and Alcohol Abuse
- Introduction to Law Enforcement
- Criminal Justice
- Fundamentals of Counseling

Business
- Principles of Finance
- Principles of Financial Accounting
- Human Resource Management
- Organizational Behavior
- Principles of Supervision
- Business Law II
- Introduction to Computing
- Introduction to Business
- Money and Banking
- Personal Finance
- Management Information Systems
- Business Mathematics

Physical Science
- Astronomy
- Here's to Your Health
- Environment and Humanity: The Race to Save the Planet
- Principles of Physical Science I

- Physical Geology

Applied Technology
- Technical Writing

Humanities
- Ethics in America
- Introduction to World Religions
- Principles of Public Speaking

AP- Advanced Placement
- Art History
- Biology
- Calculus AB
- Calculus BC
- Chemistry
- Computer Science A
- Computer Science AB
- Macroeconomics
- Microeconomics
- English Language
- English Literature
- Environmental Science
- European History
- French Language
- French Literature
- German Language
- Comparative Government & Politics
- U.S. Government & Politics

- Human Geography
- Italian Language and Culture
- Latin Literature
- Latin: Vergil
- Music Theory
- Physics B
- Physics C
- Psychology
- Spanish Language
- Spanish Literature
- Statistics
- Studio Art
- U.S. History
- World History

To be added in 2007:
- Chinese Language and Culture
- Japanese Language and Culture

SAT Subject Exams

English
   * Literature

History and Social Studies
   * U.S. History (formerly American History and Social Studies)
   * World History

Mathematics
   * Mathematics Level 1 (formerly Mathematics IC)
   * Mathematics Level 2 (formerly Mathematics IIC)

Science
> * Biology E/M
>
> * Chemistry
>
> * Physics

Languages
> * Chinese with Listening
>
> * French
>
> * French with Listening
>
> * German
>
> * German with Listening
>
> * Spanish
>
> * Spanish with Listening
>
> * Modern Hebrew
>
> * Italian
>
> * Latin
>
> * Japanese with Listening
>
> * Korean with Listening

Dual-Credit Information

Before you decide to enroll in classes, be sure to check your state's policy on dual-credit to see if you can receive reduced tuition or other benefits. The following information is taken from a U.S. Department of Education study on state dual enrollment policies. The entire study may be read online at http://www.ed.gov/about/offices/list/ovae/pi/cclo/cbtrans/index.html.

It is the most recent comprehensive study I was able to locate, but state and local laws change regularly. When you are ready to enroll, I suggest checking current policy on your state's Department of Education website, or consulting your state homeschool organization for the latest information.

States with Dual-Credit Policies

Program Features	#	States
States without dual enrollment policy		Alaska, Connecticut, Delaware, Hawaii, Louisiana, Nebraska, New Hampshire, New Mexico, New York, Pennsylvania, Rhode Island, South Carolina
States with dual enrollment policy	38	Alabama, Arizona, Arkansas, California, Colorado, Florida, Georgia, Idaho, Illinois, Indiana, Iowa, Kansas, Kentucky, Maine, Maryland, Massachusetts, Michigan, Minnesota, Missouri, Mississippi, Montana, Nevada, New Jersey, North Carolina, North Dakota, Ohio, Oklahoma, Oregon, South Dakota, Tennessee, Texas, Utah, Vermont, Virginia, Washington, West Virginia, Wisconsin, Wyoming
Must be offered	18	Arizona, Arkansas, California, Colorado, Florida, Georgia, Idaho, Indiana, Kentucky, Maine, Michigan, Minnesota, Nevada, Ohio, Oklahoma, South Dakota, Virginia, Washington
Voluntary	8	Kansas, Missouri, Mississippi, Oregon, Tennessee, Texas, Vermont, Wyoming
Mixed approach	2	New Jersey, North Dakota
Not specified	10	Alabama, Illinois, Iowa, Maryland, Massachusetts, Montana, North Carolina, Utah, West Virginia, Wisconsin

States with Tuition Payment Policies

Program Features	#	States
Students pay	7	Alabama, Arkansas, California, Kansas, North Dakota, Oklahoma, South Dakota
Institutional decision	6	Arizona, Missouri, Montana, Texas, Virginia, West Virginia
Institutions pay	11	Colorado, Florida, Idaho, Iowa, Michigan, North Carolina, Ohio, Vermont, Washington, Wisconsin, Wyoming
State pays	6	Georgia, Illinois, Indiana, Maine, Minnesota, Utah

States with Eligibility Requirements

Program Features	#	States
College discretion	3	Oregon, Vermont, Wyoming
High school discretion	6	Arkansas, California, Kansas, Kentucky, Montana, North Dakota
Joint decision	1	Utah
State requires 'proficiency'	2	Michigan, Texas
State requires 'advanced'	9	Alabama, Georgia, Idaho, Indiana, Missouri, Oklahoma, Tennessee, Virginia, Washington
Combination	6	Arizona, Florida, Maine, Massachusetts, Ohio, Wisconsin
State regulates student age or grade	17	Alabama, Arizona, Arkansas, Georgia, Idaho, Indiana, Iowa, Maine, Montana, North Dakota, Ohio, Oregon, South Dakota, Tennessee, Virginia, Washington, Wisconsin

Reproducible Worksheets

Here are the worksheets you will need in order to plan your college degree. You'll see a filled-out sample first, then a blank copy for you to reproduce and use. The **College Comparison** worksheet provides you with the opportunity to compare features and costs of several schools. You may be surprised to find that your local college is the very best deal! This is the first worksheet you will fill out, and you will see that there are questions between each section, so you will know what information is needed.

The **Degree Plan** worksheet will help you to gain a clear picture of what you need to do to earn your degree. I've provided enough copies to see you through a standard bachelor's degree, with an additional copy to reproduce in case you need more. To fill out the Degree Plan worksheet, use your college catalog to fill in the core requirements, major requirements, minor requirements (optional), and elective credits. Remember, 120 credits equals about forty classes.

And finally, the **Countdown To Your Degree** worksheet is a fun little chart I created when I was in college. It contains one square for each credit hour that is needed for a bachelor's degree. As I completed each class, test, or portfolio, I would color in the corresponding number of squares, so that I could see my progress. It's not something you have to do, but for a visual thinker, it's rather inspiring!

To begin work on the College Comparison Worksheet, you will need access to the internet, or to catalogs from each of the colleges you are considering. Once you've chosen a college, you can begin filling out your Degree Plan. You can start the degree plan before choosing a major, but you won't be able to complete it until you know exactly what you want to do.

I hope you enjoy the worksheets, and find them helpful. You may reproduce each of the worksheets for use in your own home, for as many students as are in your immediate family.

College Comparison Worksheet - Sample

College:	Sample University	Website:	www.sampleu.edu
Address:	Tinyburg, CA	Contact E-mail:	missdove@sampleu.edu
Phone:	123-456-7890	Financial Aid E-Mail:	finaid@sampleu.edu

Accreditation	Yes- WASC (www.wascweb.org)
Financial Aid Available?	Yes- Federal and private sources. Full-time students only.
Are the following items required by this school?	
High School Graduation	No- they accept dual-credit students.
SAT / ACT / AP	Either SAT or ACT; no AP tests required.
Placement Tests	Yes- math and language arts placement tests required.
How many credits are required or accepted for graduation?	
Credits for Graduation	120-132 for BA, depending on major.
Credits Earned Through the School	33
Transfer Credit Limit	99
Which of these items does this college offer?	
Portfolio Option	Yes- experiential and academic portfolios accepted.
Online Classes	Yes- over 200 classes offered online.
Independent Tutorials	Upper-level only; student-initiated.
Audio or Video Classes	No.
Which of the following exams are accepted for placement or credit at this college?	
CLEP	Yes- all subject exams, some general exams; for credit.
AP / SAT Subject Exams	Yes- most accepted for placement.
DSST	Some accepted for credit; some for placement.
TECEP or Excelsior	Decided on an individual basis (no guarantee).
List the basic cost of learning at this college.	
Tuition- Per Credit or Class	$309 per credit hour
Tuition- Per Semester or Year	Depends on number of classes taken.
List dollar amounts for each of the following fees. Some are standard, some are optional.	
Application / Enrollment Fee	$35 application.
Technology Fee	$111 per semester.
Credit Evaluation/ Transfer Fee	None
Portfolio Evaluation Fee	$200 per department (any number of credits).
Portfolio Fee Per Credit	None
Graduation Fee	$75- includes cap and gown.
Comprehensive Fee Option	None
Fill in all you can for each college. Fees may have different names, but these are the basic types.	

Get a Jump Start on College!

College Comparison Worksheet	
College:	Website:
Address:	Contact E-mail:
Phone:	Financial Aid E-Mail:
Accreditation	
Financial Aid Available?	
Are the following items required by this school?	
High School Graduation	
SAT / ACT / AP	
Placement Tests	
How many credits are required or accepted for graduation?	
Credits for Graduation	
Credits Earned Through the School	
Transfer Credit Limit	
Which of these items does this college offer?	
Portfolio Option	
Online Classes	
Independent Tutorials	
Audio or Video Classes	
Which of the following exams are accepted for placement or credit at this college?	
CLEP	
AP / SAT Subject Exams	
DSST	
TECEP or Excelsior	
List the basic cost of learning at this college.	
Tuition- Per Credit or Class	
Tuition- Per Semester or Year	
List dollar amounts for each of the following fees. Some are standard, some are optional.	
Application / Enrollment Fee	
Technology Fee	
Credit Evaluation/ Transfer Fee	
Portfolio Evaluation Fee	
Portfolio Fee Per Credit	
Graduation Fee	
Comprehensive Fee Option	

Fill in all you can for each college. Fees may have different names, but these are the basic types.
© 2007 Janice Campbell.

Degree Plan - Sample

Required Course C=Core; M=Major; m=Minor; E=Elective	How Credit Will Be Earned				Fulfilled Requirement
	Exam	Class	Portfolio	Transfer	
C & m - History				X	CSULA- Hist 111 & 112- American History
C & m - History	X				CLEP- Western Civ. I & II - 6 cr.
C - Social Science				X	CSULA- Psychology 1
C & M - Philosophy		X			MBC - Philosophy 101
C & M - Arts		X			MBC - Theatre 216 Shakespeare
C - Humanities	X				CLEP- Humanities 6 cr.
M - Literature	X				CLEP- Analysis / Int. Literature 6 cr.
C - Mathematical Reasoning		X			MBC- Pre-Calculus
C - Natural Sciences				X	CSULA- Oceanography
C - Experiential			X		Portfolio- Computer / Business Skills 6 cr.
C - Physical Education		X			CSULA- Horse Riding 3 quarters
C & M - Foreign Language				X	CSULA- Latin 3 quarters / 9 credits
C - Arts			X		Portfolio- Graphic Design 121 & 122
E - Business	X				DSST- Introduction to Business

In the first column, list one class requirement per square. Place a check mark in the column indicating how you plan to earn the credit—by exam, portfolio, etc. Finally, when you have earned the credit, make a note in the last column specifying exactly how the requirement was fulfilled (type and name of exam; class name and grade, and so forth) and how many credits were earned.

Sample Notes: Classes listed are for a student majoring in English, minoring in history. Notice that many classes or exams can fulfill requirements in two areas.

Get a Jump Start on College!

Degree Plan				
Required Course C=Core; M=Major; m=Minor; E=Elective	**How Credit Will Be Earned**				**Fulfilled Requirement**
	Exam	Class	Portfolio	Transfer	

In the first column, list one class requirement per square. Place a check mark in the column indicating how you plan to earn the credit—by exam, portfolio, etc. Finally, when you have earned the credit, make a note in the last column specifying exactly how the requirement was fulfilled (type and name of exam; class name and grade, and so forth) and how many credits were earned.
© 2007 Janice Campbell.

Countdown to Your Degree - Sample

DSST Core- Introduction to Business	CSULA Core- Science 161- Oceanography	MBC Core- Art 240 Medieval & Renaissance Art	CSULA Phys Ed. Horse Riding
CSULA Transfer for core credit in foreign language- Latin- 9 credit hours	MBC Major- English 360 Modern American Poetry	CSULA Elective- Applied Arts- Intro. to Interior Design	
	CLEP Core and Major- American Literature I & II		
	MBC Major- English 399 Spenser's Faerie Queene	CSULA Core & Major - Eng. 111 Freshman Composition	
CLEP Core and Elective- Humanities		MBC Core- Math 160 Pre-Calculus	MBC Major- English 220-221 English Literature I & II
MBC minor- History 360-361 British History I & II	CLEP Core & Minor- Social Science and History		
	CSULA Minor- American History 111 & 112		
CLEP Major- Analysis and Interpretation of Literature		CLEP Core- Natural Sciences	
CSULA Major- COMM 280 Public Speaking	MBC Core and Major- Theatre 216- Shakespeare		
Portfolio Core- Experiential- Computer / Business Skills			MBC Core- English 400- Senior Seminar

Each box represents one credit on the way toward your goal There are 140 squares, but you will probably need only 120-130 for your bachelor's degree. As you complete exams and classes, color in one box for each credit earned (an average of 3 boxes per class). You can use a different color for each method of earning credit- exams, portfolios, etc, or for major, minor, and core classes. It's your chart— enjoy!

Get a Jump Start on College!

Countdown to Your Degree

Each box represents one credit on the way toward your goal There are 140 squares, but you will probably need only 120-130 for your bachelor's degree. As you complete exams and classes, color in one box for each credit earned. You can use a different color for each method of earning credit- exams, portfolios, etc, or for major, minor, and core classes. It's your chart— enjoy! © 2007 Janice Campbell.

The Jump Start Checklist

- Read *Get a Jump Start on College!*

- Sign up on the website for the free e-newsletter, so that you won't miss new study guides and resources.

- Start studying for exams in core subjects.

- Order information from colleges.

- Fill out College Comparison Worksheets.

- Choose a college.

- Create a Degree Plan.

- Fill out a financial aid application.

- Start taking exams as soon as you are ready.

- Take classes as desired.

- Keep quality records using *Transcripts Made Easy.*

- Graduate!

- E-mail jc@everydayeducation.com to share your story.

- Enjoy!

© Janice Campbell - Everyday Education - www.EverydayEducation.com

If one advances confidently in the direction of his dreams,

and endeavors to live the life which he has imagined,

he will meet with a success unexpected in common hours.

Henry David Thoreau

Opportunity is missed by most people because it is dressed in overalls and looks like work.

Thomas Edison

Knowledge is a comfortable and necessary retreat

and shelter for us in an advanced age;

and if we do not plant it while young,

it will give us no shade when we grow old.

Lord Chesterfield

Obstacles are those frightful things you see when you take your eyes off your goal.

Henry Ford

Difficulties mastered are opportunities won.

Winston Churchill

Index

A

Accreditation, Importance of 38
Advanced Placement 11
AP 23, 44, 51, 63
Audio Resources 52
Available Exams 59

C

Challenge Portfolio 28
Choosing a College 37
Choosing a Major 40
Choosing Exams 25
Citation Methods 48
CLEP 24, 44, 51, 60
Clustering 25
College-Level Exams 23
College Comparison Worksheet 38
College Comparison Worksheet - Sample 69
College Textbook 51
Community College 34
Core Curriculum 16
Core Reading 52
Core Requirements 16
Cost of College 12
Council for Higher Education Accreditation 38

D

DANTES, see DSST 24
Degree Countdown - Sample 73
Degree Plan 45
Degree Plan - Sample 71
Degree Requirements 15
  Associate Degree 15
  Bachelor's Degree 15
Distance Learning Classes 33
DSST 24, 51, 61
Dual-Credit 65
Dual-Credit Policy Chart 66
Dual Enrollment Policies 65

E

EFC 42
Electives 18
Estimated Family Contribution 42
Exam Acceptability 24
Exam Comparison Chart 24
Experiential Portfolio 28

F

FAFSA 42
Financial Aid 41
  How to Apply 42
Free Application for Federal Student Aid 42
Freshman-Only Scholarships 43

G

Grants 43

H

History of Education 10

J

Jump Start Checklist 75

M

Major Requirements 17
Minor Requirements 17
Motivation 12

O

Online Classes 33
Online Research 48

P

Personal Organization 49
Portfolio Credit 27
Portfolio Guidelines 28
Portfolio Questions 31
Prior Learning Portfolio 27

Q

Quarter System 15

R

Readiness 9
  Academic 10
  Emotional 10
  Intellectual 9
Reading
  Book Lists 51
Reading, Importance of 20
Regional Accrediting Agencies 58
Register For an Exam 26
Reproducible Worksheets 67
  College Comparison Worksheet 70
  Degree Countdown 74
  Degree Plan 72
Resources 55

S

SAT Subject Exams 64
SAT Subject Tests 23, 51
Scholarships 43
Self-Assessment Questions 21
States with Tuition Policies 66
Study Steps 53
Suggested Subject Clusters 26

T

TECEP 24
Test-Taking Skills 49
Test Company Transcript 24
Timeline 52
Time Management 49
Transferring Exam Credit 25
Transnational Association of Christian Colleges and Schools 38

U

U.S. Department of Education 38

V

Video Resources 52

W

Western Literary Tradition 20
Writing Basics 48
Writing Skills 47
  Essays 47
  Research Report 47

About the Author

Janice Campbell is a lifelong learner, writer, and conference speaker who has enjoyed homeschooling since the late 1980's. She and her husband, Donald, have seen the benefits of home education in the lives of their four sons, two of whom graduated early from college, and two who are currently getting a jump start on college. Janice takes joy in sharing what she has learned with others. Through her home-based business, Everyday Education, Janice offers workshops on writing and on homeschooling through high school, with a focus on making the most of the teen years through early college or entrepreneurship.

Janice graduated *cum laude* from Mary Baldwin College with a B.A. in English. She is author of *Transcripts Made Easy, Zeitgeist Literature: Self-Directed, College-Preparatory, Literature-Based English for Homeschoolers,* and *Get a Jump Start on College!*; editor of *The Virginia Homeschool Manual*; and creator of the Beat-the-Clock Essay Workshop™, an innovative one-day workshop that prepares students for timed SAT, CLEP, and ACT, essays. Janice blogs at www.janice-campbell.com, and her website, www.EverydayEducation.com, offers information, resources, inspiration, and a free e-newsletter.

Order Form

Dear Friends,

I am in the midst of updating and reprinting several of these resources. Most are available online as e-books or MP3 files before they are printed, so please be sure to check price and availability on my website, www.EverydayEducation.com, before you order. If I can answer any questions, please feel free to e-mail me at jc@everydayeducation.com! Order forms may be mailed to: Everyday Education, 13041 Hill Club Lane, Ashland, VA 23005-3150.

Sincerely,

Janice Campbell

Quantity	Item Description	Each	Total
Zeitgeist Literature			
	English I: Introduction to Literature		
	English II: Literature and Composition		
	English III: American Literature		
	English IV: British Literature		
	English V: World Literature		
Help for Homeschooling Through High School... and Beyond			
	Transcripts Made Easy		
	Get a Jump Start on College! A Practical Guide for Teens		
	Beat-the-Clock Essay Workshop- Audio CDs plus Handbook		
Audio CDs			
	Homeschooling Through High School		
	Teaching Language Arts		
	Evaluating Writing		
	Paying for College		
	Microbusiness		
	Making Time for Things That Matter		
	Caring for Our Own		
	Subtotal		
	Tax (5% for VA residents only)		
	Shipping		
	Order Total		

Ship to: Name_____

Address _____

City/State/Zip _____